Eye-Opening Star Mandala Patterns Adult Coloring Book

Exquisite Star Mandalas Coloring Book For Adults

Star Mandala

By : Gala Publication

Published By :

Gala Publication

ISBN-13: **978-1522708018**
ISBN-10: **1522708014**

Design 1

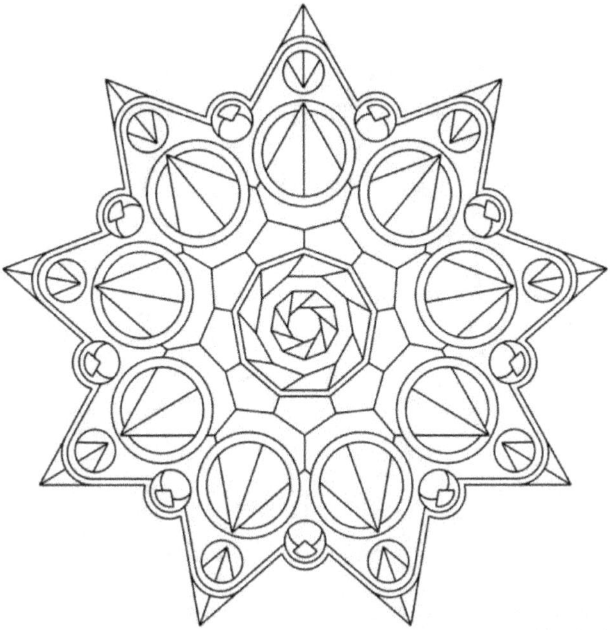

Design 2

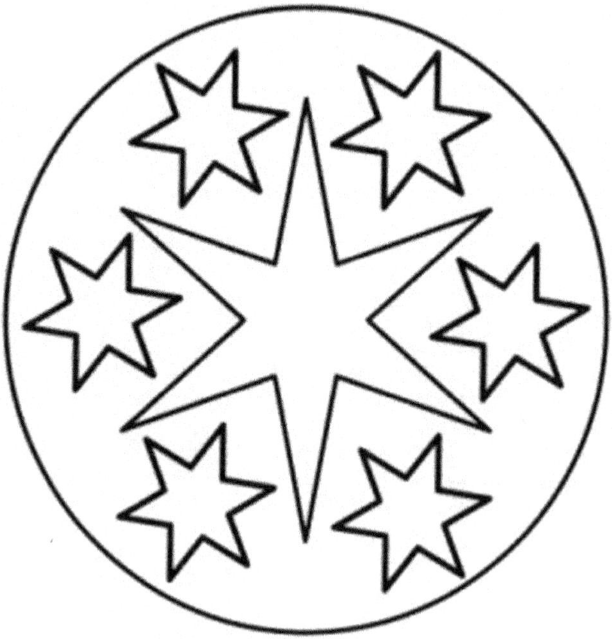

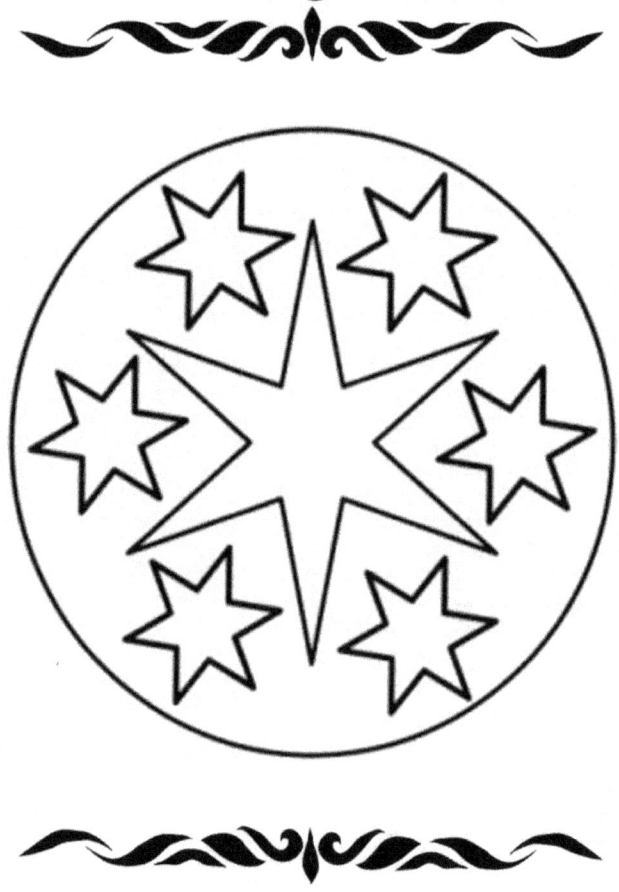

Design 3

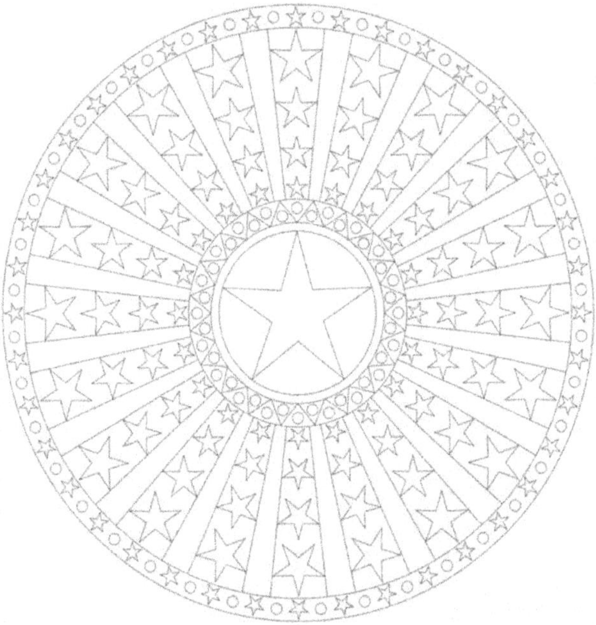

Design 4

Design 5

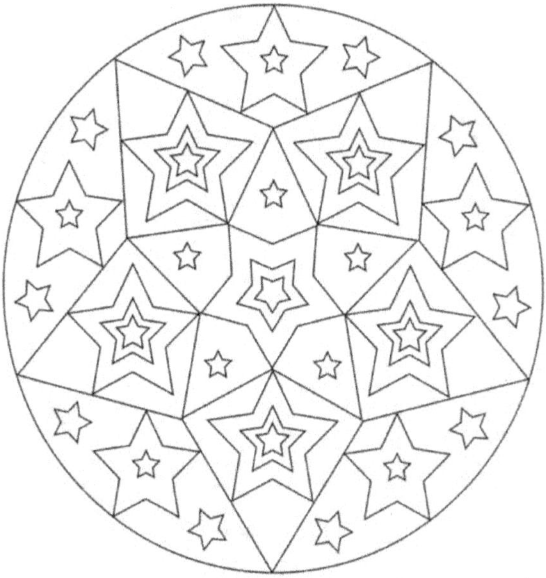

Design 6

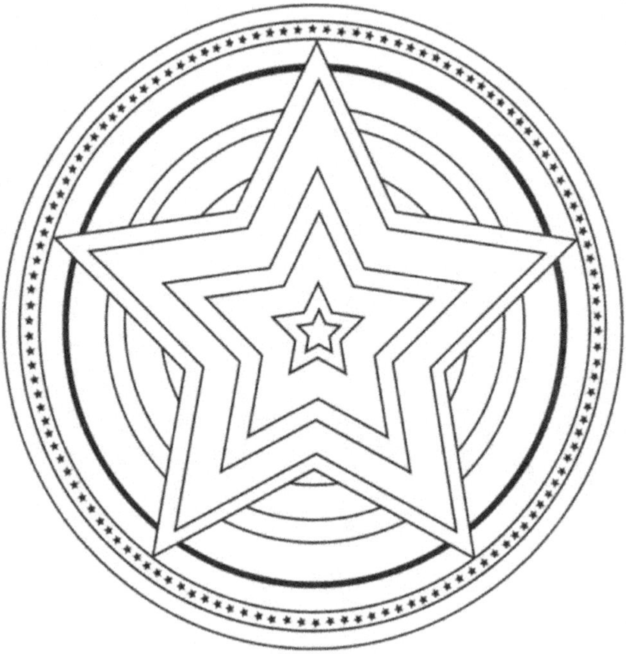

Design 7

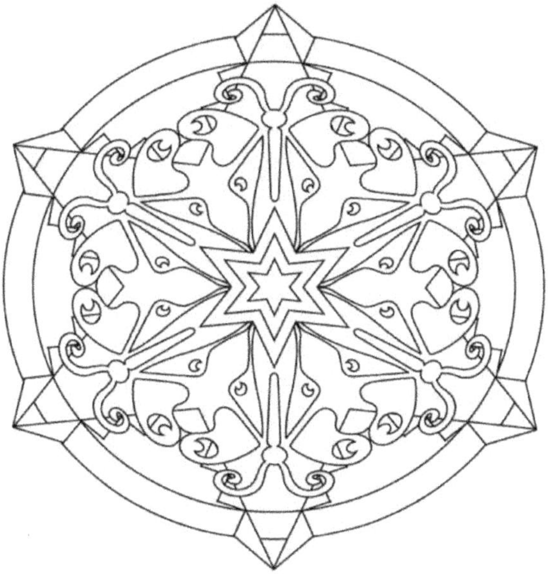

Design 8

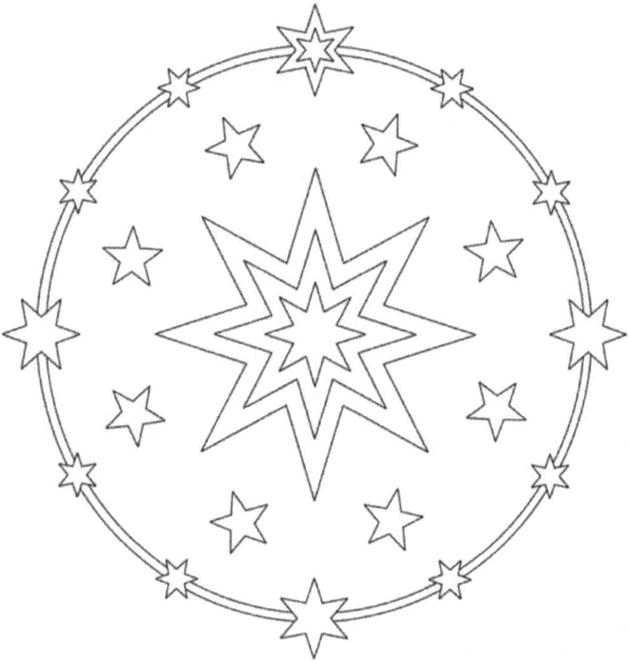

Design 9

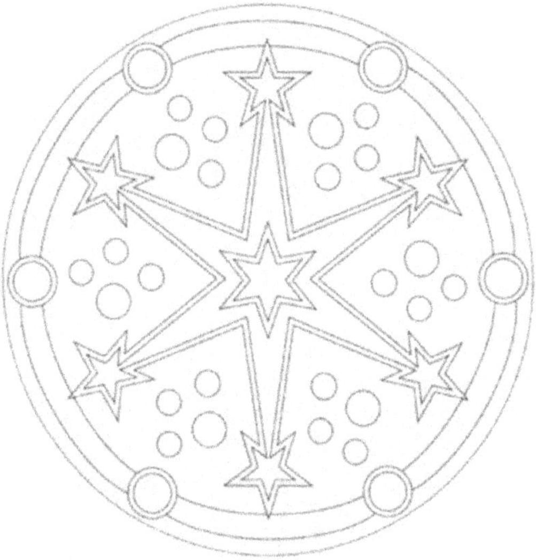

Design 10

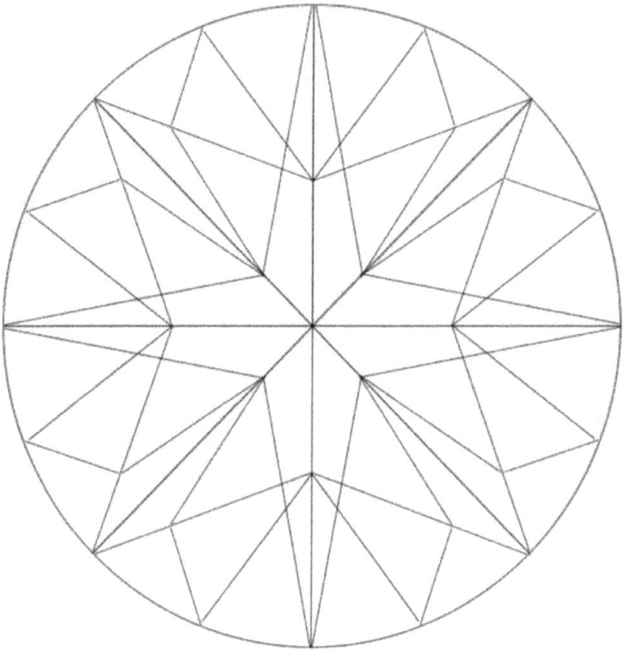

Design 11

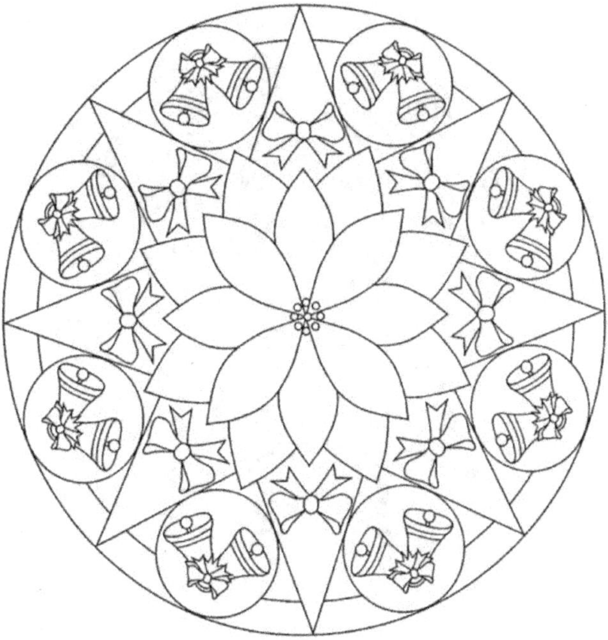

Design 12

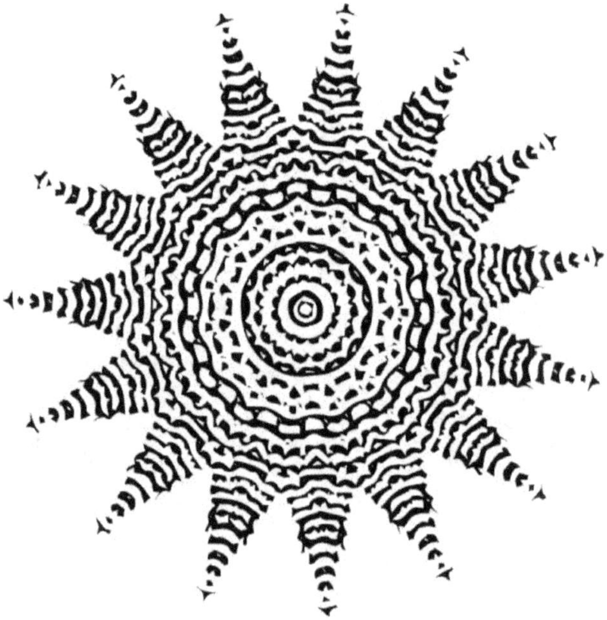

Design 13

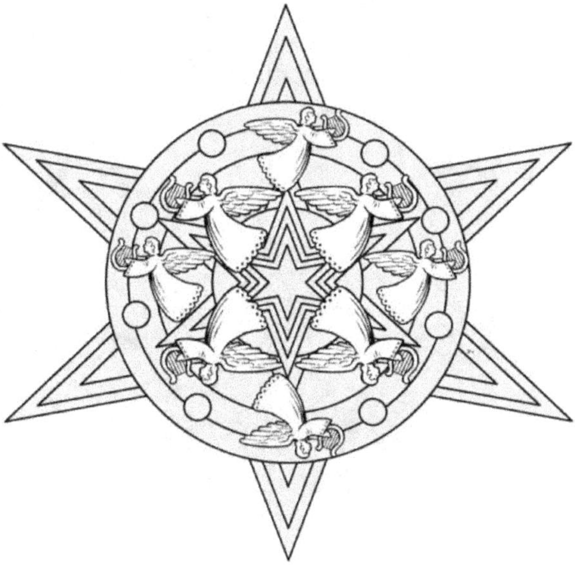

Design 14

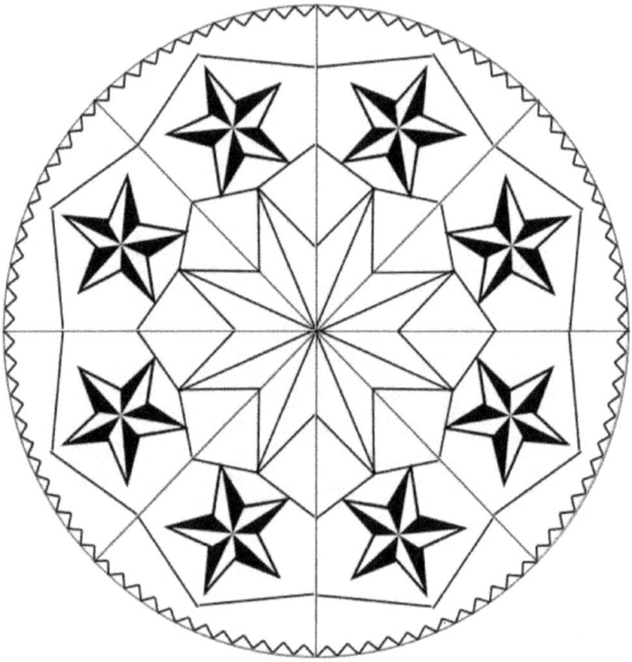

Design 15

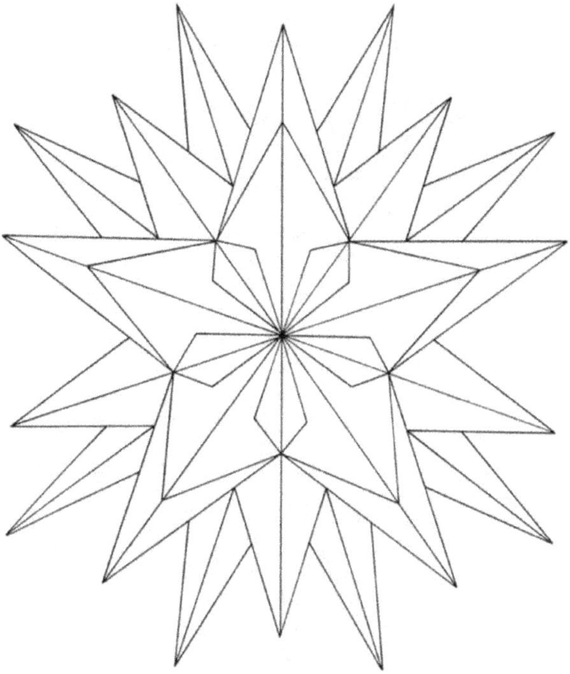

Design 16

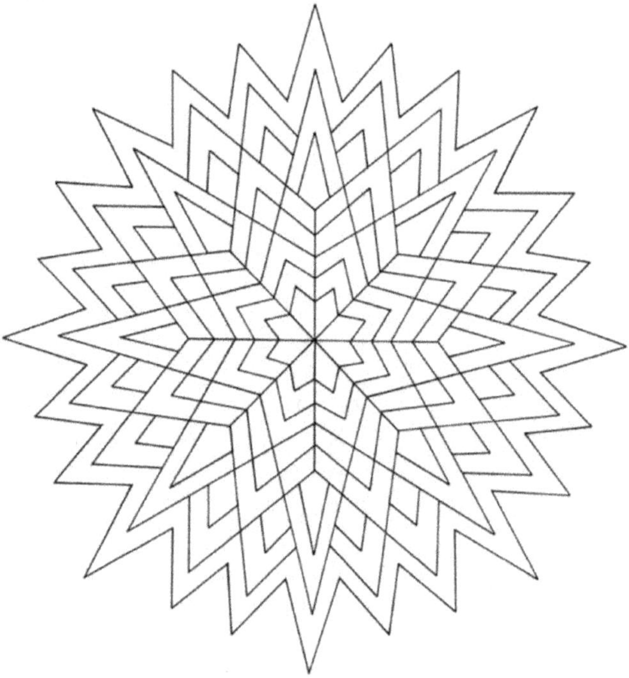

Design 17

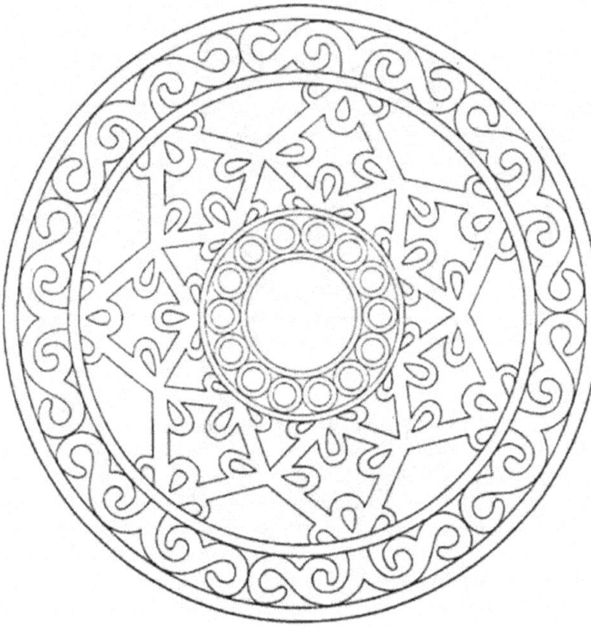

Design 18

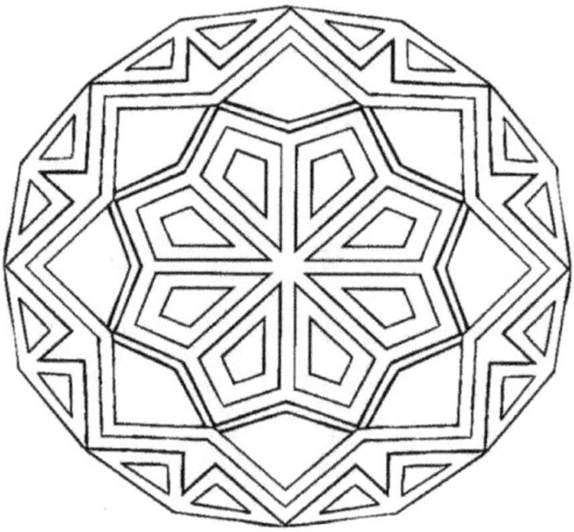

Design 19

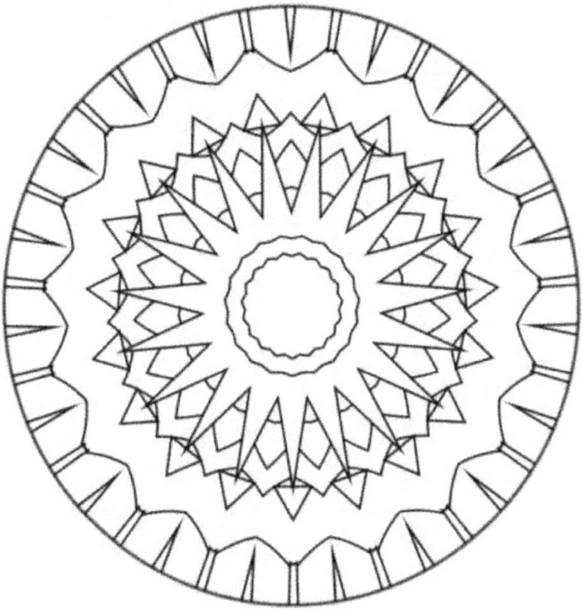

Design 20

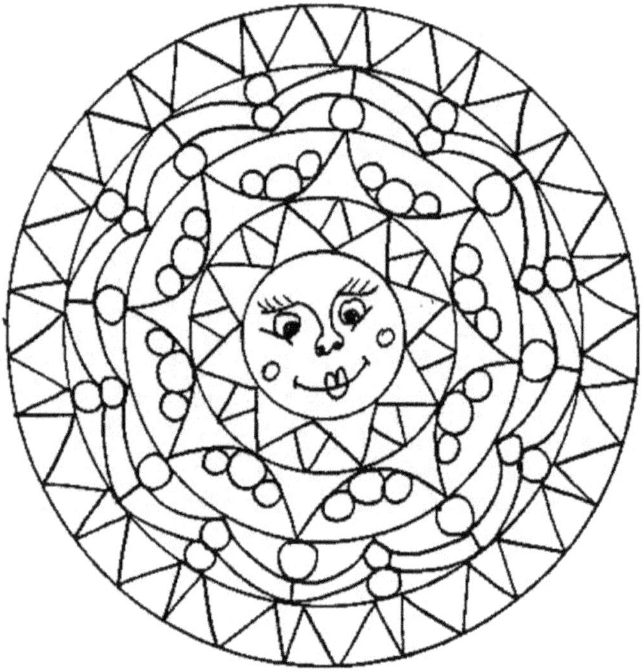

Design 21

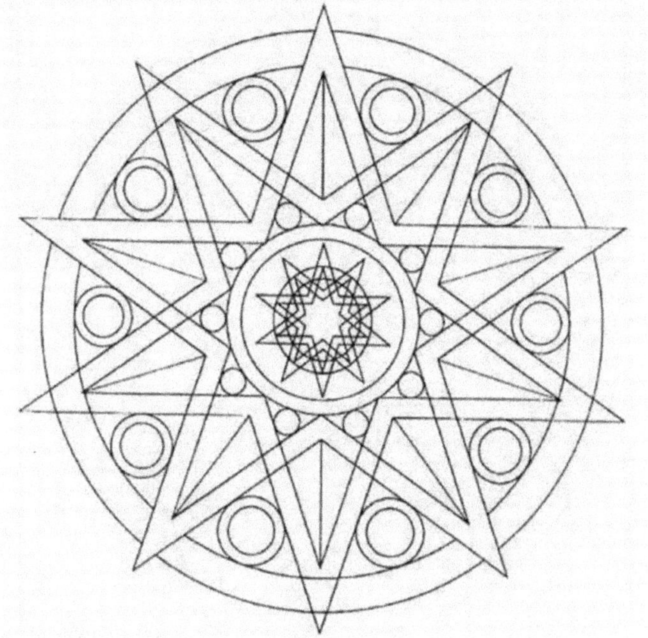

Design 22

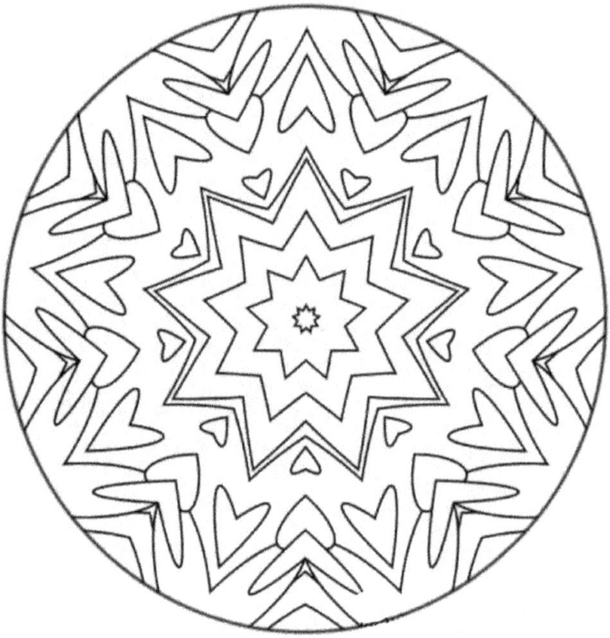

Design 23

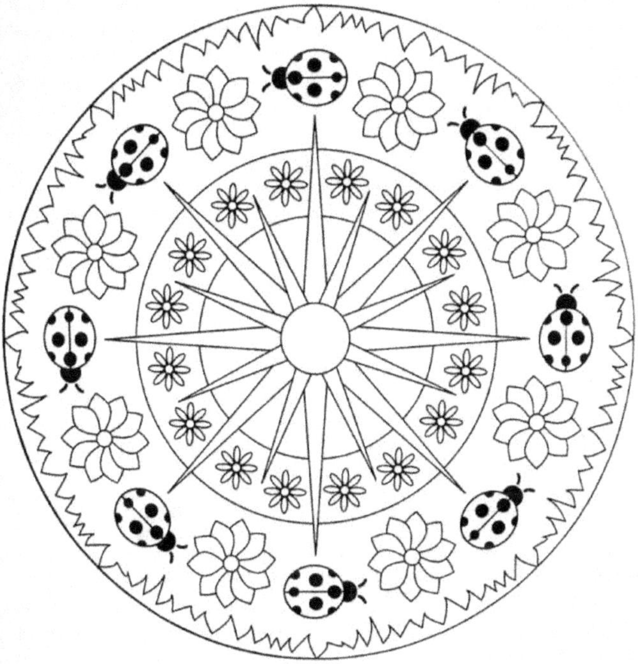

Design 24

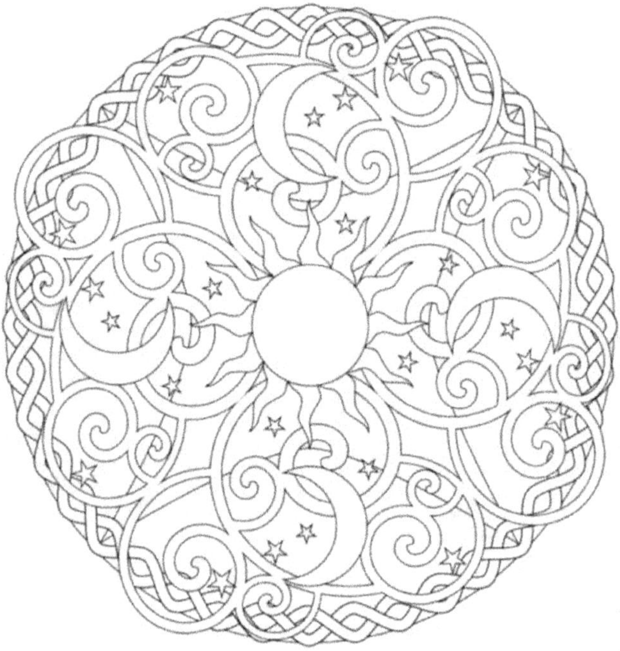

Design 25

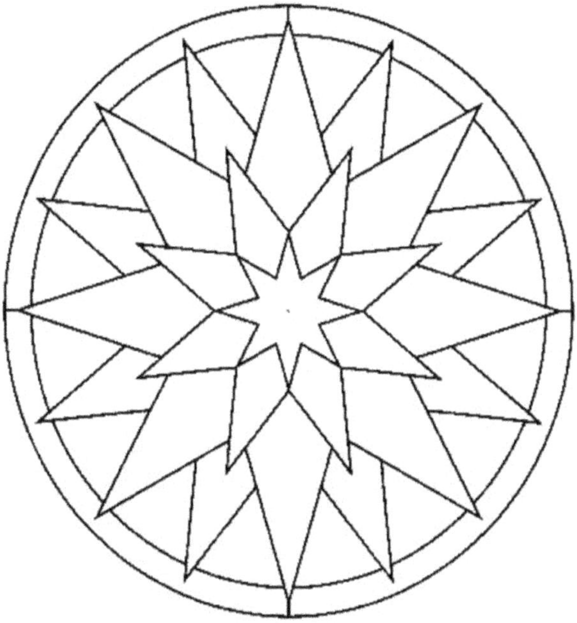

www.ingramcontent.com/pod-product-compliance
Lightning Source LLC
Chambersburg PA
CBHW071603170526
45166CB00004B/1772
* 9 7 8 1 5 2 2 7 0 8 0 1 8 *